FIRST ENCYCLOPEDIA

SHARKS

Contents

What is a shark?   4
Shark bodies   6
Breathing   8
Shark senses   10
Shark teeth   12
Hunting for food   14
Filter feeders   16
Blending in   18
Baby sharks   20
Sharks on the move   22
Unusual sharks   24
Endangered sharks   26
Megalodon   28
Glossary   30
Index   31

What is a shark?

With their super-sharp teeth, sharks are excellent hunters of the sea. There are about 450 types of shark, including the largest fish in the world – the Whale Shark.

Cartilage

Unlike a human skeleton, a shark's skeleton is made up of cartilage, not bone. Cartilage is light, soft, and flexible, which helps the shark to twist and turn when it swims. We have cartilage in our ears and our nose.

Did you know?

Unlike other fish, sharks cannot swim backwards.

Tail fin

Types of shark

Great White Shark

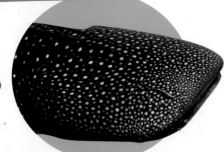

Whale Shark

Leopard Shark

Shark parts

Most sharks have a pointed snout. Some, like the Bull Shark (page 22), have a blunt-shaped snout, while others, like hammerhead sharks (page 10), have a completely different shaped head!

Sharks have a very large liver. This helps them stay afloat.

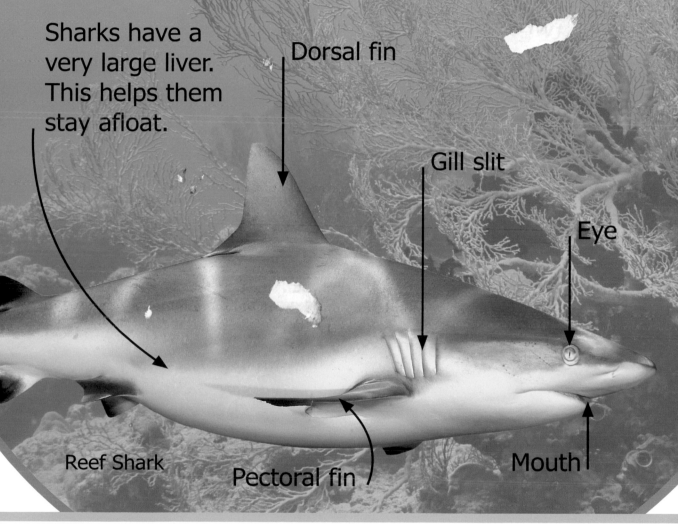

Dorsal fin

Gill slit

Eye

Reef Shark

Pectoral fin

Mouth

Hammerhead Shark

Blacktip Reef Shark

Zebra Shark

Shark bodies

Sharks are different shapes and sizes to match the life they lead in the sea. Most sharks have a torpedo-shaped body but some, like the Angelshark and wobbegong sharks, have flat bodies.

The pectoral fins help the shark to move from side to side and to steer through the water.

A shark uses its tail fin to push forward.

Super fin

The Thresher Shark has the longest tail fin of any shark!

The dorsal fin helps the shark to balance. Without fins, a shark wouldn't be able to keep upright!

A dark color on the top of the shark's body means that it blends in with the ocean.

Gill slit

A torpedo-shaped body makes it possible for the shark to swim quickly through the water.

A light color on the shark's belly blends in with the sky and helps it hide from animals below.

Tough skin

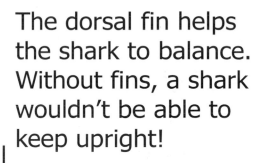

Sharks' skin is as rough as sandpaper! The skin is covered in millions of tiny teeth called denticles, instead of scales. The denticles point backwards, helping the shark swim faster.

Breathing

Sharks need a gas called oxygen to live. They use their gills to "breathe." When water passes over a shark's gills, the gills take in oxygen from the water. The gills then pass oxygen into the shark's blood to be carried around the shark's body.

Water flows out of the shark's body through its gill slits.

Sharks have between five and seven pairs of gills in their body.

As a shark swims, water flows into its mouth and passes over its gills.

Some sharks also take in water through small holes called spiracles, just behind their eyes.

Pumping water

The Nurse Shark moves slowly, so to make sure it gets enough oxygen, it opens and closes its mouth, pumping water over its gills.

Leopard Shark

Keep swimming

Like many sharks, the Blacktip Reef Shark must keep swimming to "breathe." If it cannot move, it will not be able to breathe and will die.

Shark senses

The shark is the perfect predator. It uses six senses to hunt and catch its prey: sight, sound, taste, touch, smell, and the ability to sense electricity.

Ampullae of Lorenzini

Sharks bite and taste their food before eating it.

Hammerhead Shark

Eye protection

Some sharks have special protective eyelids that close over their eyes before they attack. This prevents the eye from getting damaged.

All living creatures give off some electricity when they move. Sharks sense electricity using tiny holes called *ampullae of Lorenzini* on their head and snout. This helps sharks to hunt nearby prey.

Sharks smell through their nostrils. Some sharks can sense blood in the water up to 3 miles (5 km) away.

Most sharks have good eyesight. A hammerhead shark's eyes are at either side of its head. This allows the shark to see above and below it at all times!

A shark's ears are behind its eyes. Sharks are good at hearing very low sounds.

Shark teeth

Sharks have hundreds of teeth to help them hunt and eat their prey. Some sharks have sharp, pointed teeth, while others have small, flat teeth. The shape and size of the teeth depends on the food the shark eats.

Houndsharks

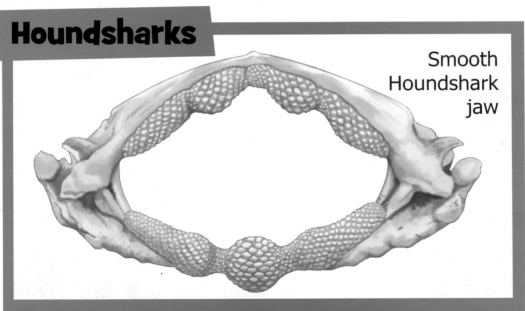

Smooth Houndshark jaw

Houndsharks have flat teeth for crushing shellfish, crabs, octupuses, and squid.

Moving teeth

A shark's teeth are arranged in rows. When one tooth falls out, another moves forward to replace it. Some sharks can get through 30,000 teeth in their lifetime!

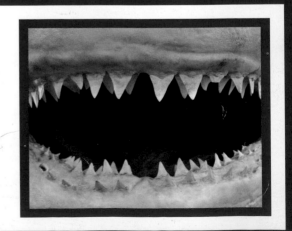

Sandtiger Shark

The Sandtiger Shark has sharp, pointed teeth for catching slippery fish.

Great White teeth

In its upper jaw, the Great White Shark has sharp, sawlike teeth to slice the meat and bones of seals, fish, and even other sharks.

Pointed teeth in the lower jaw help the Great White Shark to hold on to its prey.

Great White Shark

Hunting for food

Most sharks are amazing hunters that swallow their food whole or in large chunks. Many sharks push their strong jaws forward to grab their prey. They take a bite to injure the prey, then leave it to die before returning to eat.

Great White Shark

What an appetite

Tiger Sharks have a reputation for eating almost anything. As well as sea turtles and seals, Tiger Sharks have eaten objects like tin cans and car license plates!

Sharks can hunt at night and during the day. They tackle prey like whales, seals, sea turtles, fish, and sea lions.

Sometimes, a Great White Shark attacks its prey from below. It launches itself at the prey and out of the water completely! This is called breaching.

Excellent eater

Hammerheads' *ampullae of Lorenzini* are spread over their wide head. This makes hammerheads better at sensing their prey than other sharks. They also use their head to pin down stingrays before eating them.

Filter feeders

Not all sharks are fierce predators. The Whale Shark, Basking Shark, and Megamouth Shark are filter feeders. They all have a massive mouth and feed on tiny plants and animals called plankton.

Whale
Shark

Filter feeder sharks

Whale Shark   Megamouth Shark   Basking Shark

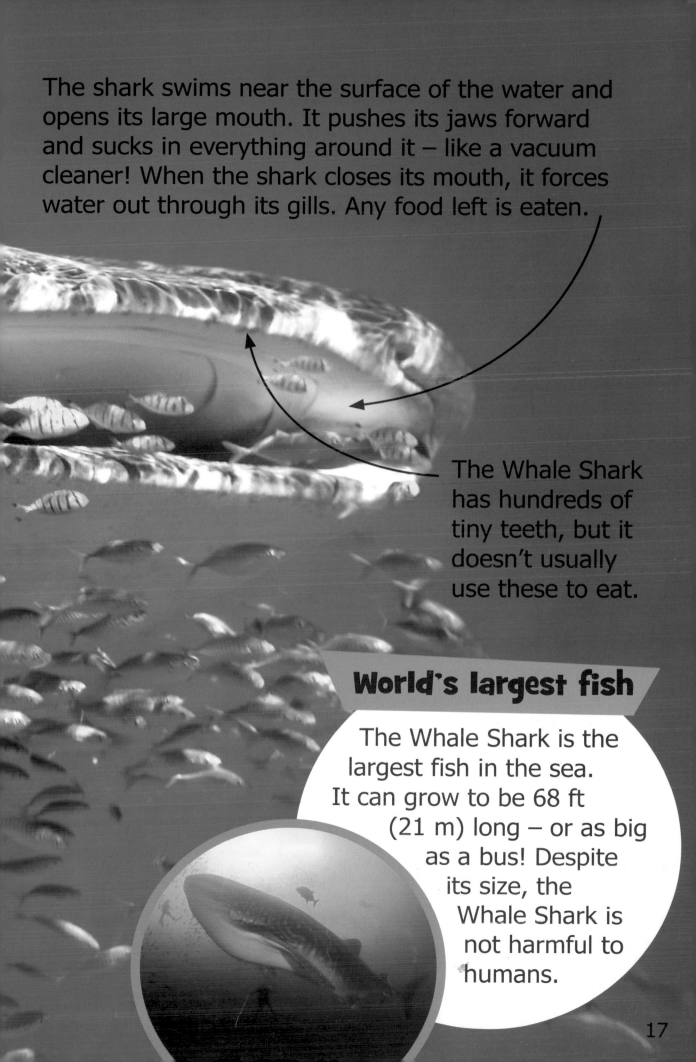

The shark swims near the surface of the water and opens its large mouth. It pushes its jaws forward and sucks in everything around it – like a vacuum cleaner! When the shark closes its mouth, it forces water out through its gills. Any food left is eaten.

The Whale Shark has hundreds of tiny teeth, but it doesn't usually use these to eat.

World's largest fish

The Whale Shark is the largest fish in the sea. It can grow to be 68 ft (21 m) long – or as big as a bus! Despite its size, the Whale Shark is not harmful to humans.

Blending in

Some sharks have patterned and colored skin. This helps them to disguise themselves and hide, so that they can attack their prey by surprise.

Angelshark

The Angelshark has a very flat body. It can be gray, reddish brown, and greenish brown in color with white spots and dark blotches. Its appearance allows it to hide on the sea floor and wait for its prey to swim by before pouncing!

Wobbegong sharks

Some wobbegong sharks have a mouth that looks like it is covered in seaweed. Wobbegongs use this disguise to attract fish towards them before attacking.

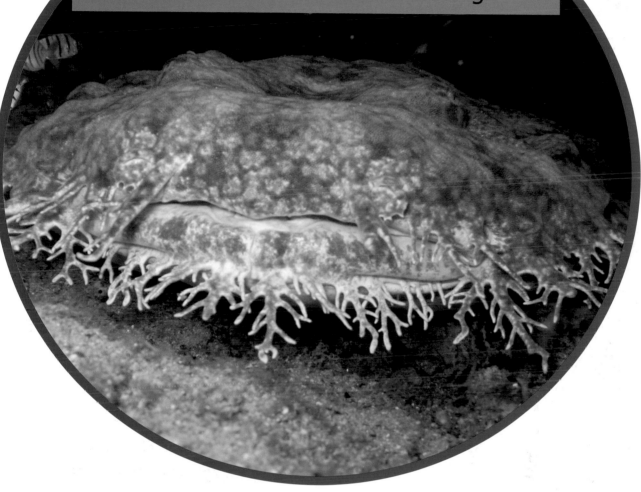

Zebra Shark

The Zebra Shark has creamy-yellow colored skin that is covered in brown spots. This helps it to camouflage with its surroundings.

Baby sharks

Shark babies always look like miniature versions of their parents. They are called pups. Different sharks give birth to their young in different ways. Once a shark pup is born, it swims away from its mother and starts life on its own.

Eggs and pups

A Sandtiger Shark mother doesn't lay eggs. Instead, the eggs grow inside egg cases in her body. When a pup is ready, it hatches out of the egg case and is born.

Lemon Shark mother

Egg case

Growing inside

Blue Shark pups grow inside their mother. They are linked together by a cord that gives the pup food and oxygen. When the pups are ready, the mother gives birth.

Lemon Shark pup

A Lemon Shark pup grows inside its mother and is linked to her by a special cord.

Shark mothers don't look after their pups. Once born, the pup has to fend for itself.

Egg-laying shark

The Port Jackson Shark lays its eggs in the sea. Each egg is covered in a screw-shaped egg case to protect it from harm. The shark carries the egg cases in its mouth and is thought to wedge the eggs into crevices to keep them safe. An empty case is know as a "mermaid's purse."

Sharks on the move

Sharks can be found in oceans all over the world. Many sharks prefer to live near to the shore in sandy bays or coral reefs, but they can travel long distances in order to mate with other sharks and find food.

Bull Shark

Some fish keep close to sharks so they can feed on any leftovers. The fish attach themselves to the shark by sucking on to the shark's skin.

Shortfin Mako

The Shortfin Mako is thought to be the fastest shark, reaching speeds of 45 mph (72 kph).

The Bull Shark has a thick muscular body. It gets its name because it is built a bit like a bull.

Dorsal fin

Bull Sharks can survive in the fresh water of rivers and lakes as well as the saltwater of the ocean. They have been seen in the Mississippi River in the United States, in the Amazon River in South America, and in southern Africa.

Gill slit

The Bull Shark has a rounded snout. It is an aggressive and powerful shark.

Pectoral fin

Mouth

Terrific travelers

Every year, Blue Sharks make long journeys across the ocean, swimming up to 5,700 miles (9,200 km). Another long-distance traveler is the Great White Shark – one was tracked swimming 12,400 miles (20,000 km) in just nine months!

Unusual sharks

Some sharks do not look anything like sharks at all. Scientists are still learning about their strange features.

The Megamouth Shark has a gigantic mouth filled with tiny teeth. It uses its enormous mouth to suck in lots of small plants and animals, similar to the way the Whale Shark feeds.

Other unusual sharks

The Goblin Shark has a long, flat, pointed snout. Unlike other sharks, the Goblin Shark has a pinkish-gray colored body.

Goblin Shark

Crocodile Shark

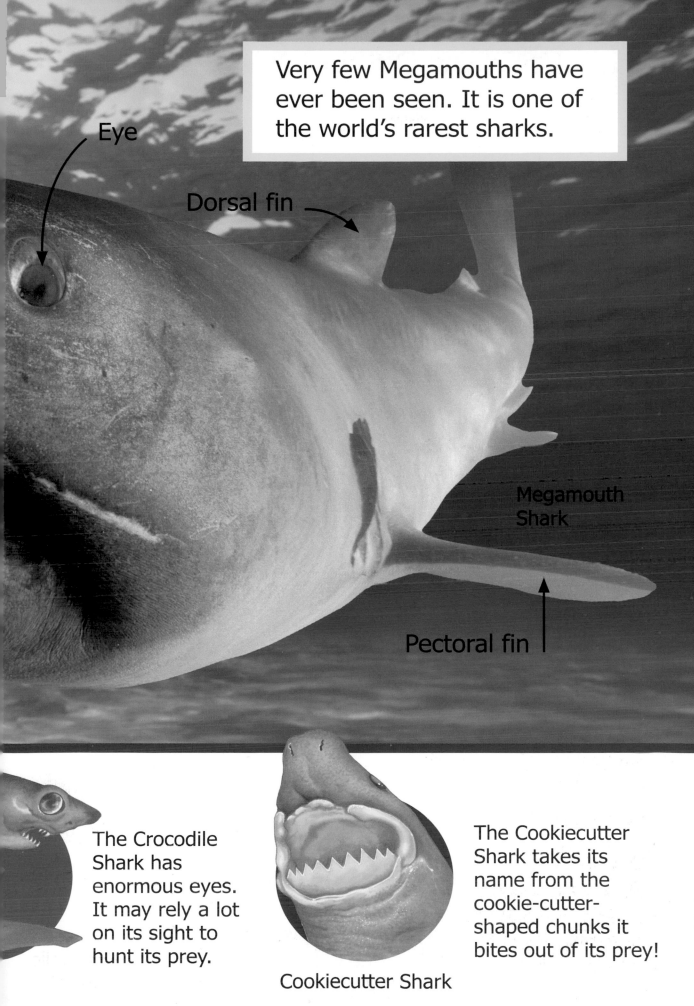

Eye

Dorsal fin

Very few Megamouths have ever been seen. It is one of the world's rarest sharks.

Megamouth Shark

Pectoral fin

The Crocodile Shark has enormous eyes. It may rely a lot on its sight to hunt its prey.

Cookiecutter Shark

The Cookiecutter Shark takes its name from the cookie-cutter-shaped chunks it bites out of its prey!

Endangered sharks

Despite being powerful predators, some species of shark are endangered, which means they are at risk of dying out completely. Some sharks are killed by pollution in the sea, while others are overfished, or simply caught by people for sport.

Shark finning

Many sharks are caught and killed for their fins – including sharks that are endangered. Once the shark is caught, all of its fins are cut off. The fins are then used to make a soup.

Shark fins

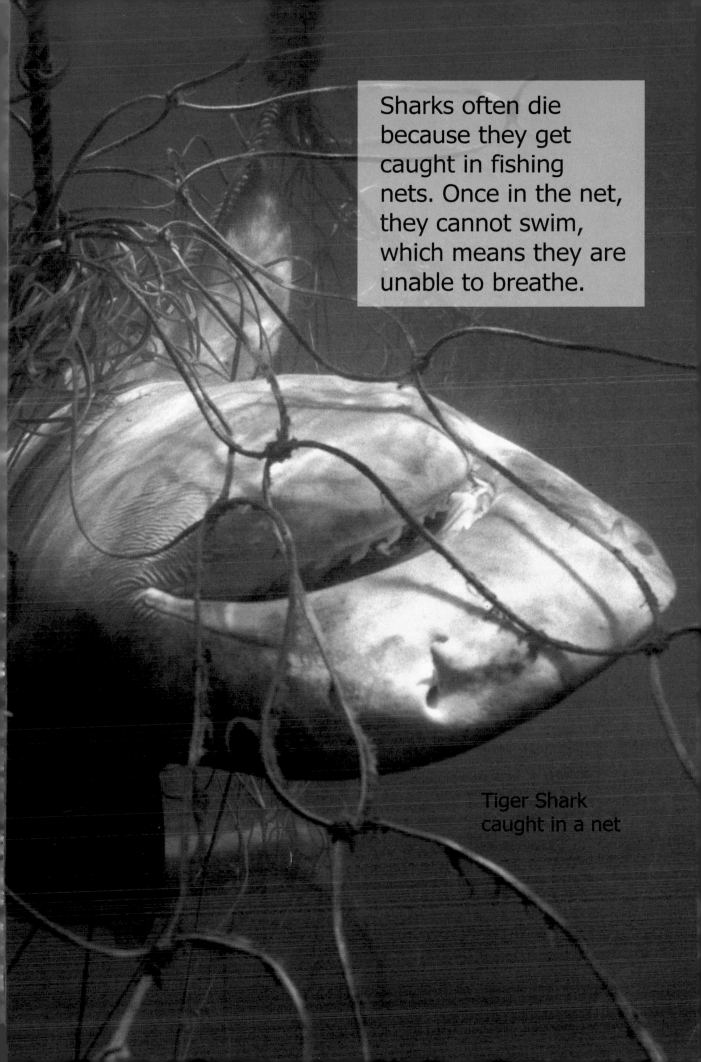

Sharks often die because they get caught in fishing nets. Once in the net, they cannot swim, which means they are unable to breathe.

Tiger Shark caught in a net

Megalodon

Sharks have been roaming the oceans for over 400 million years. A shark called Megalodon first appeared about 20 million years ago and became extinct about 1.6 million years ago. It is thought to be the biggest shark ever.

Dorsal fin →

It is thought that Megalodon ate large whales by biting off their tails and flippers.

Megalodon's massive jaw is thought to have been up to 7 ft (2 m) wide.

Pectoral fin

Mega tooth

Megalodon simply means "big tooth." So far, Megalodon's teeth are the only part of its body that has been found. One tooth can be as big as a human hand! The size of Megalodon's teeth has helped scientists to guess how big it might have been.

Scientists think that Megalodon could have been up to 82 ft (25 m) long!

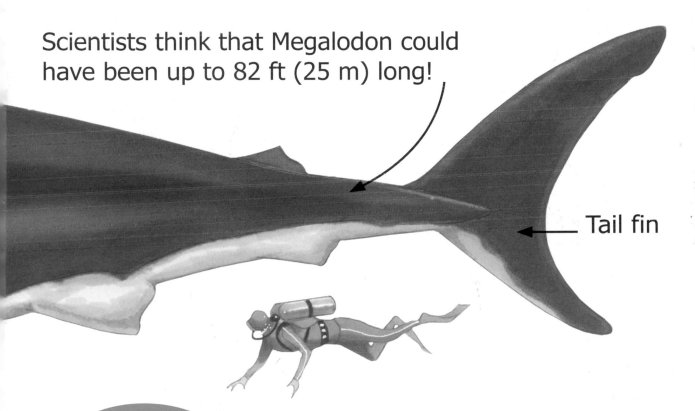

Tail fin

In the family

Megalodon's teeth are similar to the Great White's teeth. Scientists have used this knowledge to suggest what Megalodon might have looked like.

Glossary

This glossary explains some of the harder words in the book.

camouflage When something hides by blending in with its surroundings.

cartilage A tough, white material found in a human's ear, nose, and joints and in the skeleton of sharks and rays.

crevice A crack or a hole in a rock or a wall.

denticles Tiny teeth that cover a shark's skin.

disguise To change or hide the way something looks to blend in with its surroundings.

endangered To be in danger or at risk.

extinct When an animal is extinct, there are no other animals of its type alive.

filter feeder Animals that feed by sieving out small animals and plants from water.

fin A thin, flat part of an animal's body, used for swimming and balancing.

gill A body part that allows fish and other animals that live in water to "breathe." Gills take in oxygen from the water.

hatch To break out of an egg and be born.

hunter An animal that looks for and kills another animal for food.

jaw The bones that make up a mouth and hold the teeth.

oxygen A gas that we breathe so that we can live. Animals also need oxygen to live.

predator An animal that hunts and eats other animals.

prey An animal that is hunted and eaten by another animal.

pup A baby shark.

scales The small plates that overlap each other like roof tiles on an animal's body.

snout The front part that sticks out from an animal's head. The snout includes the nose, mouth, and jaws. A snout can also mean an animal's nose.

spiracle A hole in the body of some animals. It lets the animal take in oxygen.